PARTING

WAYS

Poetry by Liz

Elizabeth Schuyla

ISBN 978-1-64468-726-0 (Paperback)
ISBN 978-1-64468-727-7 (Digital)

Covenant Books, Inc.
11661 Hwy 707
Murrells Inlet, SC 29576
www.covenantbooks.com

To Kerry. May you always know how much you are loved. And to your adoptive family who were all I had hoped for when I chose them to love, cherish and care for you.

To my loving family who nurtured me through my heartache and theirs so that I was able to move forward on my journey through life.

To my kind husband who has never judged me and has always loved me for who I am.

To my wonderful children whom God blessed us with. You gave me a second chance to be a loving mom. I cherish you and thank you for giving my life so much meaning and happiness.

I love you all.

You have all been wonderful blessings in my life for which I will always be Grateful.

PROLOGUE

Thirty years ago, Liz was an unwed expectant mother. She worked seven days a week to save money for the path ahead. Once her pregnancy became apparent, she was laid off from her weekend job and due to bleeding complications in her pregnancy she was then advised to bed rest the remainder of the pregnancy. Despondent, alone and so uncertain of the future, the prospect of adoption became very real. With the help of an adoption agency Liz was able to place her daughter with a wonderful family.

Parting Ways is a compilation of not only her heartfelt expressions of being a birth mother, but of life after her daughter was adopted. Her writing was, in essence, a way of journaling. The poems and prose may require a tissue box at times, but the purpose of this book is twofold.

Firstly, may our adopted children always know how much they are loved by their birth mothers. The decision to part ways was because we wanted the best life possible for 'YOU' and you are so loved and held sacred in our hearts always.

Secondly, may all the birth mothers out there who suffer in silence with the emptiness or self-doubt they may feel, please know that you are courageous. Let go of those who feel entitled to criticize and judge, for their judgment is not your burden to carry. You are strong and brave and worthy of love and a full life.

And may birth mothers and adoptees always remember that we are strong, we are good enough and within our hearts is and always will be a sacred place for each other.

To My Family

To my family,
Who were always there for me
Through my struggle,
Your support was steadfast.
I pained you so,
As I lamented over decision.
Your hearts broke with mine,
As we said goodbye.
I was the youngest of us all,
And put you through too much.
I am sorry for the heartache I caused,
For you had to say goodbye too.
How one's decision affects those
Who dare to love another.
You have all always been there for me
Through joy and pain.
Thank you for your compassion
And your loyalty.
I love you all forever and always.

Let Go of Judgment

Judgment comes from a place
Where compassion does not exist.
Those that feel so inclined to do so,
Have not walked in the shoes of another.
No one path is the same.
Everyone's journey is diversely different.
May we all learn to accept one another as we are,
With our own truths, pains and perspectives.

May we strengthen our character with each passing day.
We are all good enough.
Dispose of the self doubt.
Believe in your worthiness.
Believe in your purpose.
Let no one hold you back.
Another's judgment is not
Your burden to carry.

Blossom in your own garden
Without the weeds of insecurity.
Love fully and look back with wisdom.
Forward is where your future unfolds.
The only one stopping you from being all you can be, is you.

Uncloak your soul,
And let the light shine through.
Forgive yourself
And forgive others

For in doing so
We find purity and freedom.
Judge not yourself or others,
For only God has that right.

The Look

The look that transpired,
While the innocent slept,
Penetrated to the soul,
I see in only retrospect.

The story that is told,
Is deep within my heart,
And will never grow old,
For within our Mother is where we start.

My baby lies full of life,
But without me she will proceed,
And experience the love and laughter of life,
God bless her while I bleed.

Many hearts were broken
While many were sewn,
But within my heart and soul is a token,
Of what was once my own.

CHALLENGING CHANGE

Change comes unexpected but not unchallenged;
It knocks but enters without answer or hesitation;
It fears no one and nothing;
But instead interferes where routine reigns.

Too often we get complacent in our ways
Satisfied with our existence
Our growth is stunted until eventually
Fear and insecurity cement our feet.

Challenges go unrecognized, ignored.
They test the part of ourselves
That we are frightened of,
Our sensitivities and vulnerabilities.

But change is progressive.
It longs to test and push beyond our
Immediate potential—further on,
Until we reach our fullest potential.

Change is not to be feared but respected.
It happens for a reason.
Although it arrives usually unwelcomed and thankless,
It never exits, unproductive.

Lost to Me

How are you?
Do you laugh a lot?
Are you a happy child?
Do you hug a lot?
What words can you now say?

These things about you I do not know,
Because of the decision made.
What things of you would I have known,
Had my decision been another.
I must admit I do often wonder
How our lives would have been together.
At times when I am successful,
I think it could have worked.
At times when I am weak, tired, and penniless,
I am thankful for the decision I have made.
The wound is still deep and exposed,
And at times I am not sure how to deal with my feelings for you.
I think of you every day,
And I always will.
I love you.
Don't ever forget that,
And, most importantly,
Please don't ever misinterpret my reasons for not keeping you.

Birth Mother's Longing

Always, within, there is a space in my heart;
Solid and permanent will you always remain;
Your heart no longer beats in sync with my own,
As it did, not so long ago;
Separately we live, but with me are you always.
Each day you come to my mind;
I'm curious as to how you are;
Are you talking—can you say Mom yet?
I long for you, I miss you, I am happy for you;
Are you like me, do you laugh a lot?
Are you happy?

You are almost a year old. Amazing.
Time has eluded me for it seems like yesterday,
When I carried you

NATURE'S HOME

The body takes the form,
Alters the shape,
To accommodate the unborn.
The breasts enlarge,
With the fluid for life's preservation.
The abdomen swells,
And aesthetically and comfortably
Houses the budding life within.
Nothing is left unaccounted for,
As quietly and most assuredly
Life progresses.
The human body, a work of art,
Of subtle genius,
In a beautiful artistic form.
It all begins so simply,
And increases in complexity
With each passing day.

HEARTACHE

It's now almost five months,
Since my baby was with me;
The lingering memory of the smell of her;
The image of her as she was and no longer is;
Her tenderness and vulnerability to the world;
So unaware of everything except hunger and discomfort;
Such things brought tears to her eyes;
Those tears so innocent.
God gave her to me, and I gave her away;
And since the day she was born, she has given happiness;
So special, so much ahead of her
The world is hers to conquer;
The world is mine to overcome.

So Quick the Day

Christmas day is here and almost gone;
The festivities are over and the gifts are unwrapped;
On the floor lies the disposed paper;
In pieces it rests, for its purpose was served;
It dressed the boxes that held the presents within;
Ribbons and bows are scattered and discarded,
Because they too served their seasonal purpose.
The tree now appears barren without those many gifts
Surrounding it decoratively.
Amazing how fervently the day progresses,
Then so quickly passes.
Christmas, as any other day is only twenty-four hours;
But yet its significance makes it worthy of being
So much longer, deserving of being so much longer.
After all, the preparation countless numbers of people
Endure only justifies the desire for the day to be extended.
But time must pass, and each day must progress;
Regardless of whether one day is more significant than
Tomorrow.

Looking Glass to the Past

The rain pours;
The thoughts flow;
Sadness fades;
And security reassures.

Life changes and rearranges;
Leaving its scars,
And the wisdom,
Of its worthwhile lessons.

A boy becomes a man;
A girl becomes a woman;
Shedding the immaturity of youth,
And the awkwardness of adolescence.

The seasons pass;
The years go by;
The memories accumulate;
In the book of our lives.

Looking back,
Our vision is clearer;
What was then blurry,
Is so simply visible.

Mistakes made;
Promises broken;
Friends lost,
Are never forgotten.

Goals achieved;
Aspirations believed;
Loved ones gained;
Are what we leave.

But always remember,
To remember;
For it is the past,
That brought us to this pass.

A Birth Mother's Heartache

They now have the baby that I once had;
Now I have the stretch marks and the swollen breasts,
That engorge periodically with the food for life,
Waiting for the recipient of whom they have long prepared for;
They drip their fluid,
Eager to be fed upon;
But she is not here to be fed;
My baby is gone.
If only my leaking breasts would stop reminding me,
Of the little life they are so eager to feed;
She is being nourished elsewhere and otherwise.
Something is wrong, it is unnatural;
For the life I carried within me,
Is no longer a life belonging to me;
She is gone, and I am left here alone with the reminders,
Trying to pick up the pieces,
When there will always be one piece missing.

EXHAUSTED

The pain isn't ending
The hurt isn't subsiding;
The loneliness isn't dissipating;
Once again I am alone,
Enduring the pain,
Hating the lack of meaning in my existence;
Why is my misfortune so pertinent to others?
I'm tired of feeling this way;
My lack of faith is becoming habit;
My innate unhappiness I hope is only temporary;
If what I did is so wonderful,
Why am I receiving no mercy;
Why does everything have to be so hard.
Something has to change.
My life can only take a turn for the better;
Because it can't get worse than it has been;
I'm tired, I'm sad, and I'm lonely and I want this hurt to end.

ONE DAY

You were mine for a day.
I could not part with you
After my hospital stay
So I brought you home for one day.
Swaddled in blankets
And cozy as could be
We all adored you.
So beautiful, so sweet, so tiny
Were you.
A bundle of miracle lying in my arms
My heart overflowed.
Held and loved by all who were there
Looking at you in your peaceful slumber.
How I look back and that time makes me wonder.
You were perfect and angelic
Barely a cry,
As if you knew that was our only time.
The parents I chose for you
Were waiting to be your mom and dad,
But for that day you were all mine.

Passing Time

Time is going on so quickly now;
No time to reminisce and reflect;
It was just yesterday,
But yesterday is already a month ago.
The life I carried within me for nine months,
Now sustains and supports herself;
I miss those feet that made my ribs move;
Those long, delicate fingers that poked at my sides
That tender head that rested between my bones,
Now rests in another Mother's arms;
The two hearts that beat within me then,
Is now only one, my own.
She grew within me,
Now she is growing without me.

A Man's Strength

A strong shoulder to lean on:
A consoling embrace in which I can feel no harm
Can possibly come to me;
Reassuring words with real meaning;
The smell of masculinity
As well as the feel of it;
Someone who is stronger than me
On whom I can abandon my fears,
And who will accept my temporary insecurities;
Someone else to deal with my problem
Besides me.
Before I crumble
I need someone there to catch me;
To rescue me from my own exhaustion;
To sweep me up and carry me
Into solace and peace of mind
Far away from this emotional beating.
His image is clear in my head
But his reality is light years away;
His accessibility unknown.
I'm tired of being so strong
So resilient and occasionally humorless;
My strength wanes
As does my elasticity.
But I know I will make it
Because I have to.
With or without those strong hands
To carry me.

UNAWARE

Conceived in heartache;
Birthed into tumultuous times;
Given away in sadness;
Growing up in war;
So young,
Still an infant;
No cognitive understanding of the circumstances,
In which she was born and is now being raised;
May the hardships which she has endured already but unaware,
Never trespass in her territory again.

MELANCHOLY

A tired dancer slumps against the wall
It is her only support these days
Yet still her lithe shape is beautiful
Despite her exhausted state
Yet still she is strong
Despite the weariness.

A young child cries in despair
He wonders why youth is so difficult
His one dream is to fly
But his wings are broken
His heart is heavy
His engine in need of fuel.

An old woman longs for youth
She was beautiful then
Her face and figure, flawless
Those who once pursued her, deceased
She is alone and despairing
Time has passed and left its mark.

A young man is heartbroken
His love has left him
He searches for answers
But only more questions arise
He is strong yet he feels so very weak
She was his strength, he realizes.

A young woman longs for her lost love
They were beautiful together
She had to leave him
She was frightened
And never again could she give all of herself.

TEAR

The tear rolls down my cheek
It follows the curve of my face
And follows the line of my lips
The taste of salt.

These tears are so easy to come by
Their source is endless
So is the sadness and the fear
Does the sadness cease.

The sun refused to shine today
And so did my soul;
My spirit had no wings like the pheasant I saw.

It flew high above what it feared, most human beings;
Do I fear them as well
I cringe from their touch
And shun their love
I find faults before strengths
I trust no one and respect few.

I prefer to be alone
Then in company
When I'm in the dark
It's so difficult to see the light.

I used to give of myself so freely
I smiled, I laughed, I believed, and I trusted
Where did I go wrong
When will I be right again.

ALONE

Alone again
Am I waiting or just searching;
Admittedly lonely but not unhappy,
Just dissatisfied.
So young in old eyes
But too much has transpired in my life
Too much to possibly regret
If I choose to do so.
My last days of twenty-three
And the worst must be behind me Already.
I've loved and lost
And given away what I loved the most.
Will the void always remain;
The mature pain Only a woman knows
The hurt I have already known
The anger I have already felt
The frustration that has caged me
In a helpless state.
The broken wings have healed
But the strength to fly
Still evades me.

Darkness to Light

Does the darkness ever end
Does it show mercy
Does it waken into light
Does it ever stop overtaking the soul
Does the darkness ever die
Does it get so deep that one drowns
Or does one float on in its murk
Enveloped until it entangles the spirit like weeds
In a marsh
Until sight and breath are gone
And the only darkness that remains is peace.

CHAINS

May we break the chains that hold us fast;
To the memories of the past,
Too long do they keep us bound,
And remorse so easily found,
One cannot long for what can no longer be,
For like a scared doe time does flee,
With no remiss of times or people past,
Time simply sets up its sail and mast
Leaving its trace scattered around
Until only memories quickly abound
Passing gracefully without hesitation
Intolerant of delays or mediation

HEARTBEATS

The bitterness fades
The hatred dissipates
The anger soothes
Into something easier to handle
With the sound of the unborn heartbeat.

What was so difficult to believe
And so hard to comprehend
How easy it was to hate
To mistrust and disbelieve
Fades as the murmur of life becomes so clear.

But with the beauty
Comes the hurt
The reality of a decision thought made
To keep or to part
With the sound of that heart.

Strength acquired
And absolutes assumed
Lose their backbone
As life gets larger
And that heart gets stronger.

My own heart aches
To think of the decision
That must be made
When the time comes
To keep or to part.

It cannot be easy
There is no right answer
There is no wrong answer
When the two hearts that beat within me now
Once again is one—my own

BECOMING

Sometimes it is so hard to see
And you wonder if that day will come
When you will become all that you can be
The self-doubt, hurt flow free
Making laughter so scarce
While you remain feeling so lonely.

Life at times is so unpredictable
And after all its curve balls it
Sometimes seems so unbearable
Love is lost and no new one found
And hope and desperation constantly abound.

You wonder if people care
Or are they just there
To remind you of days happier or sad
No two minds are alike, nor spirits nor souls
But is that the excuse for the distance that remains.

You wonder for the meaning of life
Days untouched by anything worthwhile
Do you just exist
And so little self-expression among bleeding hearts.

Enclosed in a cage of your own
With the help of society and your own inhibitions and mistakes
Colors in rainbows and sunny days aren't as bright
And clouds are meaner and darker as feels your heart
But you find solace in that because no one
wants to be alone in his darkness.

FRAGILE FLOWER

I saw a wilty flower with a wilty head
It looked as though the sun had scorched it
And the wind had been too strong,
Inconsiderate of its fragility,
Sitting on the porch with surrounding blooms
They beamed but this flower waned
Too affected by the brusque nature of fall
Too weak to sustain itself as people brushed by
Disregarding the exposed vulnerability
I tried to lift its head and speak tenderly to it
but it only looked downward when
I released it, and it resolved itself to passivity

PICTURES

Pictures reveal all;
The hidden emotions expose themselves;
The pain can't be hidden;
The happiness can't be concealed;

The rugged years leave their marks;
The wrinkles are captured;
The aging over the years is truly shown,
as I pass through the pictures.

One has chronologically progressed;
The other has just grown older;
One's youth still shines through;
The other's has passed her by.

These pictures reveal the truth;
For they catch the eyes;
And the eyes cannot lie;
The happiness, the sadness, the pain, and the loss.

Quickly Goes Time

Days gone by running into years;
The days meshing into each other;
No distinctiveness, no clarity;
Night to day, day to night;
Months evaporating, condensing into years.

So much changes, so much transpires;
Successes and failures in the memory of our lives;
Brighter vision from learned lessons;
Regrets from poor decisions;
Destiny only knows where life leads.

Time passes without consideration;
Life rearranges and before I know it,
I'm living what was once my future;
My then existence, is now my past.

Childhood, adolescence, adulthood, old age;
The cycle through which we all pass;
Our irreversible destiny that leads us on our path;
Please guide us along oh steady companion.

JEKYLL AND HYDE

Amazing how people change
So unexpectedly and so drastically
As Jekyll became Hyde so do the ones you know
Become so unfamiliar
Some may always seem to have the best of intentions
But before you know it they are gone.

Paths

At times the road becomes so windy
Detours, forks, stops, yields, and dead ends make further
Decisions so difficult
Which way to choose
Shall one follow the overgrown path or the path most recently
Treaded by another's feet
Differing possibilities lurk beyond
But one doesn't know until that path is chosen
And that decision is made
Foresight is for prophets
Intuition though is more common among mankind
So may the traveler through life use that gift
To its fullest capacity
And choose wisely and bravely
So the road chosen holds within its miles
The many pleasant experiences and opportunities that life offers.

CRY

Cry in despair It cleanses the soul
Grieve when necessary for afterwards the good times
Are appreciated even more,
And are valued more,
Cry, cry, cry
Let it out
The deluge of sorrows
And the pain
The loss
The fear
The regret
The hatred
All which grew abundant
And approached unannounced
And unwelcome
As do weeds in the midst
of a luscious garden
Choking out the life
And the beauty
Overpowering the roots
Strangling out the goodness
Which itself was once in abundance;
The precious fruit
The beautiful flowers
Gone, Lost.
The lesson to be learned Simple:
Don't allow the weeds to overtake;
Instead, overcome.

CONSTANT CHANGE

Looking out onto the same place,
For twenty-six years I have looked upon the same thing,
But have always seen it from different perspectives;
My moods have brightened or clouded my vision;
But in reality that spot has only changed with the seasons.

I reminisce to my past years of youth,
How carefree, and refreshing, yet always challenging;
The laughter, the joy, the tears, the pain,
Finding my identity through it all.

Moving on is always hard to do;
Saying goodbye to youth and irresponsibility,
Only to substitute maturity and obligations;
Life's problems surround me, but so do his arms.

Amazing how life goes on, new generations,
That fill the void that you just left;
They repeat your life in their own way;
They live life differently, but it's all the same.

TRUTH

May we always see who we are
for it is in truth that we succeed.

May we share our inner strength
for it is in doing so that we grow.

May we never long for the possessions of another
for the possessions of one's own mind and spirit are truly valuable.

May we look beyond the facade of ourselves
and strive to brighten the light from within.

May we dream for the future
for the past is evanescent.

May we wish for the best upon others
for it is in selflessness that we find satisfaction.

Most importantly, may we love
for it is through love that we find happiness.

LONGING

I'm thinking of you little one How are you?
Not a day passes without a hundred thoughts of you.
The smallest occurrence strikes the chord
Which releases a geyser of vivid detail and emotion.

Your perfectly formed body
And those attentive, aware eyes.
From the day you were birthed
I doubt you missed a thing
The eyes that looked through me
You knew everything
Thank God they were closed
in sleep when you left my life.

I doubt I could have let you go
Had you been looking at me.
God's little angel
With you went a part of my heart permanently
Severed from me as was your umbilical cord
Linking in life the two of us.
We looked at one another
As soul mates meeting for the first time.
You were so fragile with soft hair and skin
Beautiful.
From day one you subtly demanded attention.
You are loved by all whose lives you touch
And always remember, and never forget
That those who met you first
Love you more than you can imagine.

INDECISION

Lost in a world of my own thoughts
Lost in a world of confusion *indecision*

Waiting, hoping for a better way
Wanting, going for a better way

There has to be a way out
Not so painful
Decisions aren't decisions anymore
Just painful options
Winning gets so hard to do and losing,
well it just comes naturally

Wish for a better day
when love is easy
and life isn't so hard
Happiness is real
and sunshine is everywhere
It will come again

ALONE

Alone again,
Decisions made, but not necessarily well made.
Settling for less, never reaps good results.
So many gifts, and what has been done
with them thus far?
Squandered away until they slowly dissipated
Snatched in young adulthood
And slapped with the penalty paid by the irresponsible
Abandoned by a boy who only appears to be a man.
It's too late to say I should have known,
I did know although I was a fool to believe what
He told me and for believing in another person I now pay
It's a warped world and I've lost faith in myself and in others.
Will I ever trust again, will I ever love?
Most importantly, will I laugh and be happy?

I Need You God

Indecision makes me crazy
It wreaks havoc in my mind
What do I do?
What do I say?
I heard things only get harder
Is it true?
Am I destined to be unhappy?
I thought the worst was over
Then the worst descended upon me
This too will pass
But what follows?
Worse things?
It cannot be
For surely I cannot survive
My will, My spirit will surely die
Why such tests?
Are they so necessary—
Only to prove our worthiness?
I long for peace of mind
I wish to laugh again
To discard my acquired cynicism
To see the goodness that once existed
And not just the evil.
These are the dark days
God are you there
Or am I alone
I need you more than ever
For I am shutting

Myself out to others
Not intentionally
It just seems to be happening
1 am isolating myself
Trying to be an island
Withdrawing from touch
And love
The person I'm becoming
Brings tears to my own eyes
Who am I?
What happened to the goodness
I used to feel?
Is that too gone forever?
What has become of my short life?
A problem unable to be solved
A spirit weighted down
Sinking deeper
As does a brick dropped
Into the bottomless waters
Please someone catch me
Before I drown in my own reality
Please, because I want to live again.

REFLECTIONS

The past comes peering through;
The voyeurism of my conscience reeks its weakness;
The soft music brings back the tears,
Opens the door of my memories
So they may all come rushing out;
Flooding my head once again;
The acquired strength dissipates
As the flood reinforces the weakness;
So much we hide, we conceal;
to the naked eye of another there only appears
satisfaction
Their blindness is almost laughable;
So much they think they know about me;
More wrong they have never been;
So much they have yet to know;
But how much more have I yet to learn,
To go through;
What will be the ratio of pain to happiness;
This I have always wondered;
Will my sun outshine the rain;
Will happiness outweigh the pain;
I have always thought myself so pensive;
Contemplative of destiny, of fate;
Are they significant or reckless inventions;
I want to laugh unaffectedly;
To be happy and not self-conscious anymore.

May we always speak our peace
For it is in doing so that we find release
From those feelings, emotions, and regrets
That hold us fast,
And constantly impede our progress from the past

Life is by far too short to live in longing
to make things hard that could be easy

Rain

The rain falls so effortlessly
It goes where it feels the urge
And runs down the window
As tears run down a cheek
Slowly but effortlessly too
When the hurt is felt too deeply.
The clouds rain themselves out
And then disappear
Revealing blue skies
Just as you cry yourself to exhaustion
Only to realize there is laughter
& sunshine to make you smile again

ME AND YOU

Me and you
Together alone
To face the future
And the unknown.
Separate we'll be
But one in unity
As we were
When you were mine.
Our hearts beat together
For a time.
I'll always love you
And to me
You'll always be mine.
Live completely
Don't look behind;
For it is your future
That will let you shine.

SEA

She walked alone
Her footprints vanishing behind her
In the fragile sand
The cool water washed up around her ankles
Refreshing, soothing
So many had walked that very beach before her
And so many will do so after her
But would they ever appreciate it as she did
The solace
The feeling of unity with the vast
Expanse of the sea
And everything in it
The peaceful coexistence of sea, land, and air
And herself.
The waves generated strength
A strength symbolic of so many things
Its strength never faltering as do humans
As does she
Yes it is moody;
It rages at times
Engulfing anyone and anything daring to test
Or overcome her strength.
The sea, the waves have little mercy
For they have no conscience
But at other times She is calm;
Waves merely lapping quietly, gently
On the shore;
Welcoming, not foreboding,

The sea so effected by other elements;
A product of her environment
As are we a product of our environment.
Pollute the ocean
And in return exists a contaminated cesspool;
Pollute people
And the product is a contaminated individual;
The parallel is both simple
And devastating
But only humans
Are capable of contaminating both sea and themselves
The sea does not contaminate humans
Unless we first contaminate her.

TRUE FRIENDS

To two of the few true friends
We laugh together
And reveal our hearts
Help one another
Always close-by in times of need.
When one or the other's heart does bleed
We clank beer mugs
When we're acting like slugs
And exchange thoughts and ideas
while the tab does exceed.
We've all cried to one another
About what hurts
And laughed ourselves to tears
While inhaling too many beers.

Romance

The essence of romance
It is here and soon vanishes away
So sad to see it go
So sad to long for what is lost
To grieve what can no longer be,
To love to love;
Is in itself a Sure death
We are destined to be alone
In a world full of madness
A world full of isolation.
Few find the truest of companions
They are so scarce
They are so rare
but they too long to be loved
And held closely
As a newborn is held close to the breast;
We are alone in this world
But it is our choice to be alone
Everyone longs to be loved
But everyone fears the heartbreak
And everyone fears the isolation
But do not be afraid
But reach out and touch
For you will be surprised to find
How many people, strong and weak alike,
Need to feel needed
And need to be loved as you do.

MUSIC

The music?
Yes, it is soothing;
Each note traverses
The tunnels of my existence;
And each bass sound
Pulsates and synchronizes
With my own heartbeat;
Its power is dominant
Yet its influence is subtle;
Amazing how each instrument
With its own distinctive sound
Comes together with others
So beautifully in unison
To create a new resonance;
Memories intertwine
With the melodies;
And aspirations soar
With the crescendos
As tears fall
It smooths the rough edges of life
And brings character
To the silence.

REAL FRIENDS

Friends are more precious than a diamond
True friends are more consistent than Big Ben;
Real friends love you despite your faults or faulty decisions;
Friends love unconditionally;
They ask for little in return for all that they give
And they do give all that they are capable of giving;
But in all the giving it never seems like much to them;
but to you their giving is never-ending;
And when one gives to a friend it is effortless and natural
As the eagle that soars with such ease;
And the expanse of air in which the eagle finds himself
Is comparative to the vast loyalty, love, and sharing of
Self that a genuine friend is capable of giving.
But a genuine friend is not always easily found;
And as the eagle learns to fly so do people learn how to
Be a friend, for to have a friend one must know how to be a friend
The eagle falters as we all do trying to prove ourselves
Worthy of friendship;
At times we fail, even fail miserably;
But friends forgive and if they do not, they themselves will
never learn to fly like the eagle.
And if the offender continues to repeat the same or similar
Mistakes then he/she too will never soar
But if we learn from our mistakes, as is the case in perfecting
Most things that we will become the person, the individual,
And the friend we want to be and have.

Inspiration

Inspiration is hard to define
It is found in a smile
Or it can be found in the midst of a difficult situation.
Just when one is held fast with fear, pain, or heartbreak
It may wash over like a satisfying breeze on a sweltering day;
It calms the nerves and uplifts the spirit;
It makes the seemingly unachievable appear less frightening
It makes the unbelievable, believable
And it brings color where there is none
It sets free the soul
Which has been held captive in thick darkness.
The smallest things in life may bring inspiration
Things that are free, that are naturally beautiful,
people that have overcome, children that bask in happiness,
and elders who reminisce about "the good old days."
Inspiration is everywhere if we choose to see it
Although it is hard to see when the world is weighty
But that is when we should most feel its therapeutic power
If we can't find it, inspiration may find us first;
It will pick us up and teach us to walk forward
again as a new child takes her first steps
It will turn the frown slowly into a bright smile;
And the darkness in our lives will dissipate like the
clouds of a vicious storm and once again the
brightness that once existed will shine so totally again.

MIRROR

M irror, why do you lie?
Or do you tell the truth with careless disregard?
Or does this face conceal the aged heart and mind
hidden beneath the mortal youthfulness of young flesh.

Wrinkles reveal wisdom achieved through the years
Gray hair reveals the battle against aging and
the fleeting existence of youth;
Arthritic hands and joints reveal the
determinance of years passed and their battering ability;

    A sad heart reveals the passage of time with more unhappiness than glorious days, or maybe just a longing for the years gone by.
    But no one can prevent the passage of time, for it is evanescent and inevitable.

    In youth, we long for childhood; and in adulthood, we long for youth. In old age, we long for our young adulthood. Is it vanity that holds us fast or the easy access of so many things that accompany being young? Laughter, love, acceptance, happiness. Does life get more overbearing with age as life's simple pleasures become so scarce and hard to achieve? Does responsibility overtake our natural instinct to laugh and be free? Does every small decision made come with overbearing consequences, and is depression a natural instinct or a learned trait? The smaller pleasures in life become so hard to find in the muck of reality, and when they are found, are they pursued in our better judgment or a means of immediate gratification?

Mirror, what is it that you reveal—the truth or do you lie? My left becomes my right, and my right becomes my left. You surely only reflect an image, a likeness physically to the looker. What of the interior do you reveal? Do you search the eyes and see beyond or merely reflect them? Do you feel what the looker feels, for if you do reflect the truth, then you must with little ambiguity.

Or as my right becomes my left, does the outside reveal the inside?

STRUGGLING WITHIN

Life's struggles at times seem so unfair
No one seems to care
And the meaning of life seems empty and bare
With each problem arises another
until life seems almost unlivable
And you just want to hide and take cover because life at times is so
unbearable.

Nothing goes the way it should
Children cry and people lie
Loneliness wanders aimlessly
Especially amongst those who deserve better.

At times sunlight is blinding
And bright smiles are not even sunny
At times the only bright place is where you choose to hide.

But then you see a crippled child
And you realize all you possess
There's so much strength in kindness
And so much to be gained in giving love.

We all want to be free of life's burdens
And reap its benefits
And when giving and giving is too much to bear
Keep hanging in there because for every rain there's a rainbow.

LONELINESS

Sadness lurks;
Memories ache;
Hurt reigns free;
Inside of me.

Will peace be found;
And tears be scarce;
Will smiles be abundant;
And fear be rare.

May regrets be few;
And happiness plentiful;
Will lessons be learned;
And the remains of my heart be salvaged.

I long to be free
From the heartache that binds me
From decisions poorly made
And friends poorly chosen
From loves lost whose memory continue to haunt
Waiting and living in want
For the comfort and solace found
In the arms of a man
Who can love as he once did love me.

Loneliness stripped me of my defenses
Leaving me vulnerable to the hands of darkness
Tears flow like raindrops and sobs shake the body

As thunder shakes the earth.
The storm seems eternal and so does the pain;
But the clouds rain themselves out
As the distressed heart cries to exhaustion.
A sunny day at times follows,
And at other times a gray day may ensue.
But even if another cloudy day does follow,
May the lonely soul intuitively realize
that there will soon be sun again.

Tranquil Sunset

The day wore on into the twilight;
Soft light streams through the windows;
Unobtrusive and silent, yet peaceful and protective;
Inducing solace and restfulness.
Little can mimic a sunset;
Nothing is worthy of the power it holds;
Capturing the attention of all who see;
And just when one wants it to last forever,
It fades behind the mountainside;
Tauntingly its magnificent colors linger;
Never to repeat itself as it has just been seen;
Its next performance to be dramatically different;
Its audience anxiously awaiting nature's temperamental artist.

So Close

Three towns away from me
Is where you grew up.
Knowing you were so close,
Was so heartbreaking at times.
I observed from afar
Like a guardian in the background
Not sure what to do
So as not to confuse you.
Our lives were so intertwined
Even after our time when we were combined.
Hard to believe how things turn out
How you were kept in my world
As if to quell my self-doubt.
More than you know, I was there
Seeing how you progressed
And grew from the girl
To the woman you are today.
It was so hard but yet reassuring
Knowing that you were blossoming
In your world of stability and love.
At times I know you resented me
For you could not understand
My reasons nor genuine intentions
But that time has passed
Allowing healing which takes its patient time.
You were always with me
Whether you knew it or not

I was cheering you on from afar
Always wanting the best for you
As did I then, when I said goodbye.

HURTING HEART

Memories invade my mind;
Take my peace away;
Leaving me stripped;
My defenses lulled to sleep,
By the short reprieve,
Pain, sorrow, regret
Never heal;
They just scab,
Ripped off by a careless move,
A thoughtless gesture;
This murky world,
So much confusion
You can barely see through it.
Why so hard?
Why so much loss?
Why so much pain?
Tell me why.

WINTER COMING

The trees are bare;
The skies are gray;
Winter makes its entrance;
Fall takes its leave.
Another season, another year;
Time passes so quickly,
Things change so much;
Nothing is ever the same,
With each passing season.

BELIEVE

Believe,
Believe in yourself;
Believe in others
For we are all in it together.
Know your strength within,
for it is there waiting for you to realize,
Ready to be awakened.

You are the master of your will,
Let not doubt hinder your progress.
You are powerful.
Never doubt what you are capable of.
Greatness lies within,
waiting for you to open the door.
Be gracious and open it wide.

You are talented in vast ways.
Thank the Lord for your gifts,
and never forget from whom your blessings come.
When things feel overwhelming,
remember there are others suffering
in ways your heart knows not.
Embrace your challenges.
They will lead you through the path
intended for you
to Greatness.

Our life is our landscape.
Hills, plateaus, mountains, oceans, rivers, and valleys.
We navigate our way through,
Knowing where we want to go,
but not aware of the storms ahead.
Strong winds and hurricanes may blow you off course,
but believe in yourself and that God
will always keep you on course to your true destination.

Happily Ever After

Where is my happily ever after;
What happened to fairy tales,
Do they really exist
My sadness feels it must persist.

Hurt, heartache and disappointment
Have rained on my story;
When will sunny skies
Break through the clouds
and hear my cries.

Those you love,
Whom you cherish dear;
Have turned their backs,
Betrayal
Has left you empty.
Spiritually, emotionally bereft,
Like cement shoes
Dragging you to the bottom
despite flailing efforts
to get some air.

Scathed, odd girl out;
This can't be my fairy tale.
Prince Charming
is a character
I do not know,
He was supposed to hold my heart tenderly.
Instead
he hurt it beyond repair.

POETRY READING

The courage, the talent, the beauty of what you express
In front of all, you let your soul undress
From within your heart you tell us your story
Have you any idea its beauty and its glory.

Trembling hands hold your masterpiece
That shines of who you are and where you have been
You share what is your sanctuary within
Your hidden grief, your joys, your histories and hurts
Do find their way in your poetic works.

So generous of you to let us in
Have you any idea how brave you've been
I feel as though I know you intimately
Having heard your work of art read to me.

To the Parents of My Baby

To you I unintentionally played God;
I bequeathed to you the life you were not able to conceive;
I carried her and loved her while she was mine;
She thrived within me as I suffered over decision;
Each heartbeat made her closer in spirit to me;
Each kick and motion made her presence within me even more alive;
She brought me sadness, but even more so she brought me joy;
It is with you that I chose to share this joy of her life;
For the things I could not give her, you could;
The dedicated parenthood shared by two,
Instead of the frazzled single Mother I may have become;
I know you will provide for her every need,
The love most importantly, the support, and the necessities;
She is deserving of the best—that is why I chose you;
For I myself would not have been capable of giving her
All I wanted to lavish upon her;
Never would I have wanted her to feel as though she was a burden,
Due to my sleepless impatience;
Please love her the best you know how;
And please do not be afraid to let her know that the woman
Who carried and birthed her,
Loves her and holds her sacred in my heart and soul forever.

YEARS GONE BY

Of age's ills you do decry;
years have robbed you of vitality;
Time has left you more alone;
Once so zesty and alive,
Now you just stare at the phone.

The path of life once a luscious journey;
Full of sunshine and laughter;
Has led you down a darker road;
Twilight lane has suddenly found you;
With sunset avenue not far ahead.

Do not despair, you are truly cared for;
The ones who love you are always near;
Your stars at night, your sun at dawn;
Live for what you have, not what you yearn for.

Be youthful in thought, despite your aches;
A new generation must sail in your wake;
Share what you know without grief and despair;
Life would not be the same without you there.

SHATTERED GLASS

Shattered glass, shattered everywhere,
How do you mend
A shattered glass?

Pieces strewn
In places unseen,
How do you find,
Or replace what is lost?

A new glass is not the same,
It appears as that,
But does not hold within,
What once existed.

Pieced together with the utmost care,
Shards will always be missing,
It will never again be
What it once was.

REALIST

A realist—
What one becomes
After life's experiences
Not easily defined
Different for all
A culmination
Of the good
And the bad;
A continuum of events
Unpredictable,
Happy, yet sad
Exciting and dull
Never the same
But occasionally repetitive

Involuntary Solitude

Modern-day Loneliness
Solitary, pensive
Life is simply pastel colors
That run into one another
Without any real distinction
Romance is scarce
And the well of love
Existent but unused
So hard to reach out
When all that seems safe
Is to retreat within
Eager to trust
Yet unable to do so
Wanton of love
But unwilling to risk to lose;
Wanting to connect
But exists only uncommon ground
and dissimilar ideals;
Truth becomes tainted
And honesty, rare;
Loyalty, recognized only
By one's own blood;
This loneliness enwraps
As does a quilt in winter;
Both protective and isolating
Warmth from the cold
Until true Spring
With its flowers and sunshine

Bring smiles and laughter
And the soothing radiance of the season
Is the gentle touch
Of one who is loved
And loves.

LOST LOVE

She saw him there
Arms open to her
Longing to hold her close
And draw her near
It had been so long
And so much had happened
Since they were last together
How could it ever be the same
As beautiful as it had been
Back then
Why had he called again
Maybe he knew how she
Had been holding on
No one had satisfied her
Like he did
Their love had been rich
It had been romantic
But yet now they were two strangers
Trying to renew the past
Bring it back and relive its existence
Was it possible
Could it be done
What they had
Could never be forgotten

DAFFODIL

A Daffodil rises alone
but boldly,
Defying the harshness,
Its buds announce bravely,
That it is time and I am here;
No mind to the cold that still surrounds it.
It proclaims its beautiful color and strength,
Because it is time to rise,
No matter the weather or circumstance.
It is always a promise that the warmth
And new birth of Spring is within our grasp.
It is symbolic of new beginnings,
to be embraced in a garden,
That will follow,
With beautiful flowers,
That want to be like that Daffodil.
Bright like the sun!
And so shall you be my friend!!

Separation of Spirit from Body

Slowly life leaves them.
Their bodies shut down,
The spirit parts gently;
Movement becomes less frequent;
Their eyes become expressionless;
Days pass and hope fades.

The phone rings,
But the conversation has already been heard;
For it has played before in my mind.
The drive to the hospital;
Behind the curtain lies the shell of my brother;
He has left us to deal with our pain.

Mom takes her hand,
But she pulls it away; her last breath is close,
But she still pulls away;
So little peace, so much pain;
She leaves us to our memories.

A week of loss;
A lifetime of pain;
One old, one young;
They lay side by side,
In their eternal rest;
Never again to be seen, or heard, but to be always loved.

Parallel of Death

As they lay there,
Life slowly escapes them
Their spirit gradually pass,
Waiting for their final release.

Parallels of death,
They lie there helpless,
As loved ones stand by,
To touch and to comfort them.

Why at the same time,
Does God reclaim them,
Their souls to be His,
Their bodies to belong to the earth.

Unto dust they have returned,
Free from their worldly prison,
Their spirits are released;
Their souls are in rapture.

We only are left,
To deal with the loss;
Missing links,
In the chain of our lives.

God, be good to them,
They were good to us.
We miss them,
And in You we trust.

Temporary Sanity
and Tranquility

The wind blows gently the curtain;
against the pure white column;
The fire burns effortlessly;
The peacefulness of night is magnificent and solitary.

Pervasive thoughts are now invited in;
The mind is a vast plateau;
Or a spectacular, azure, and calm sea;
A breathless sight from a mountaintop.

All that was bad is now tolerable,
All that pained my heart is less bitter;
All that I long for is within patient grasp;
All whom I love are right here beside me.

CHANGING TIME

Time goes by so quickly;
So many things change;
So many people pass through your life,
And so many things rearrange.

Time is of the essence,
Yet there seems to be so little present;
What's to become of us,
When we are in reality so evanescent.

Friends lost and found;
Love scarce or abounds;
So much in life to live for;
Smiles, happiness, laughter, frowns.

Amazing how life proceeds;
Little consideration for where it leads;
Who are we to stand in its way;
For its itinerary takes no heed.

I'M SORRY

Ode to Love Lost
Hearts I broke
Love I choked
For fear of loss
And hate of pain
In youth I walked
From a young man's blame

Now looking back
And reading through letters I stacked
I feel for those
Whose hearts I froze
You loved me complete
But instead I fled
And left you behind
To pick up the shattered pieces of your hearts.

I'm sorry today
For you from whom I strayed
No real reason I went with my feelings
I'm sorry I didn't think of you
Or include you in my plans
as I moved on into uncharted land.
You were good to me
And loved beyond my faults.
Thank you for your belief in me
But my whimsical nature led me astray

To My Parents

I love you both more than I can possibly express
For your anniversary I would only like to verbalize
the love I feel for you two who have always been one:

The most wonderful people I know are my parents;
You raised me with love and patience and selflessness;
You saw me through the rain,
And showed me how to enjoy the sunshine,
Gently you taught me,
Even when stubbornly I resisted;
And when I strayed, you tenderly reminded me of my valuable roots.

Your patience was saintly;
And your anger, rare.
I always trusted you,
But stubbornly insisted on finding my own way;
Without you though, I never would have made it through
The overgrown path that has tempted me;
But with you I have grown,
And it is you who know me the best.
Thank you so much for all that you have given me;
And even more so, thank you for the patience
you have graciously endured on me.
I LOVE YOU MORE THAN WORDS CAN EVER SAY! AND THANK YOU
for being all that you have been to me.

PHOTOGRAPH

The smile says one thing;
But the eyes say another;
Amazing what is revealed,
In the power of a photograph.

The intensity can't be lost;
The laughter, a temporary shield;
But the mask is stripped,
When the eyes shine through.

The innocence of infancy;
The laughter is generous;
The smiles are so brilliant;
The eyes shine with warmth and love.

With the progression of time,
The years shed their age,
On the faces of the old;
The eyes reveal what the wrinkles can't tell.

Broken Man

Sightlessly he stares
The vacancy within is apparent.
At one time his light shone brightly
Too much pain, too much hurt
His heart, his soul are sucked into the quagmire

He leans on his cane
Looking out upon the vast ocean
He longs to laugh
To see a child smile upon him.

Full of dreams was he
But life had other plans
Fate lured him seductively
Away from choices he would/could have made
A past that should have been his own.

Little time is now left
His life soon to be parting
He will quickly be forgotten
Or so he feels.

In each other's dreams they meet
But dawn rips them apart
Her long wistful hair
His strong broad shoulders
their warm embrace vanished with their arousal

On a distant shore she reflects on her life
So short yet at times so painfully long.
Where is this man she has dreamt of so often
Why this longing for a man she does not know
A phantom who steals his way into her night

Too old to be feeling this way
Too used to being alone to invite another in
So youthful in her dreams
So old in reality.

MAN IN A WHEELCHAIR

You remind me of all that is good in life
I don't know you

I see you in that chair restricted in all you can do
How I wish I could sit there for you
And allow you to stand

You are more special
words can't justify your dignity and beauty

You have warmed my heart
Rekindled my soul

DANGEROUS

Struggling to break free
Of your conniving ways
I saw what you were
What you are and will always be.

Never again shall I venture so close
To one as untrue and false as you
Your ends have no respectable means
Awaiting your next prey alone you will be.

Ensnared one day you will surely be
When your prey one day overtakes thee
Like a black widow to sit and wait
For an innocent victim to take your bait

Spider's Glossy Web

The fabric is so shredded
There is nothing left to sew back together
You've lost me forever.
My heart aches for you
My heart aches for me.

The decision is made
Too late to turn back
You're cold, you're ice
Your false affections no longer suffice
Like a quiet motionless spider
Beckoning to me
Your allure
You drew me in
Your glistening web entangled me.
I tried to get close
But saw your shiny web too late
You there waiting to strangle me slowly
with your devious ways

MY PRECIOUS CHILD

Little feet trudge their way
Through the grainy sand
Amazed at every sight and sound
He encounters along his way

The wind whips around us
A gentle breeze not found
Yet he makes his way joyfully
Because it's the two of us

So young yet he's come so far
A bundle of dependence
Has already found his way
No doubt in my mind he will go far

To feel such overwhelming love
My heart aches at what's ahead
Protect him from pain and heartbreak
May he only experience laughter and love

A child now, a man tomorrow
God guide me in my motherhood
For he is so tender and impressionable
Make him whole and strong for all his tomorrows

INNOCENCE LOST

Loss of the innocence;
Dissipated;
And then was gone;
Without a final "goodbye";
Leaving me behind;
A woman, not a child anymore;
The responsibilities of an adult;
No longer the reckless abandon of an adolescent;
Decisions that leave a woman happy yet sorrowful;
Pain only a woman can know.
The innocence is gone forever,
Never to return...
Sometimes I want it back;
Even more so lately;
But I trespassed beyond the boundaries;
And have lost the innocence,
In order to become wise.
A loss to gain,
Only to gain a loss.

YOUTH SO QUICKLY PASSING

Youth,
Pooof. gone;
With no chance to argue;
The contrast of two pictures;
The years between,
Told in the expression.
The eyes;
They tell all;
The wisdom,
The pain,
The love,
The hurt, the years that transpired;
Leaving their toll.
The first photograph;
Unknowing of what lies ahead,
The innocence of youth,
The uninhibited laughter;
The insatiable appetite to live;
The unquenchable thirst to love,
And be loved;
So much ahead;
So much yet to experience;
Only the basics left behind;
The real learning still ahead;
The harshest and the sweetest of life's experiences,
Surprise in the untraveled path ahead;
Time proceeding undaunted;
Unable to stop;

No choice but to become an adult;
No slow transition,
Just a sudden metamorphosis;
Drastic, not subtle;
A single experience incenses the change;
While future occurrences merely influence.
The eyes see the difference;
No one's soul is shielded by their own eyes;
They remain true;
No matter how deceptive is the mind;
The eyes are altruistic;
The years told in a second picture;
No more flirting with fate;
Maturity replacing innocence;
Wisdom replacing blissful ignorance;
Each experience accounted for,
In the depth those eyes.

ANONYMITY

Anonymity in the city streets
Hide away from probing eyes
So many people, so few words
Upon these streets one wears a cloak of anonymity

So many faces, so many footsteps
Somber and sightless they clickety clack past
Fear of who dwells within
prevents visual contact and emotional connection

I love and hate
This cloak of obscurity I wear heavily
Unseeing eyes are yet a relief at times
Unscrutinizing

My Inspiration

Unknowingly you have so warmed my heart.
I stood behind you looking for a seat
Then saw you there confined to your mechanical chair
If only I could offer you my legs for one hour, one day, one week.

In your metal prison you sat
While your friend read your work of art
A poem about music so beautifully flowed
Like an orchestra so brilliantly led
From her mouth but from your heart came
words only your soul could tame

Your grace, your poise, your greatness, your beauty, so tangible
Despite your chair you have so much more than anyone
Your gentle smile portrays your pride
Not boastful or gloating but genuine as the warmth in your eyes.

You brought tears to my eyes that night
Because again in my heart did shine a light
Rekindled by someone as true as thee
Have you any idea how you have affected me.

BEACH

S trong Waters, Stormy Soul

Fall days at the beach
unpredictable and serene
Furious and mean
Turbulent and everlasting

The water rushes to and fro
Reclaiming what we think we own
Bridges and buildings will never promise
What Mother Nature will never bestow

Her magnificent and temperamental ways
By us will never be tamed
Only by God, the moon and stars
Will she comply and harmonize

So little do we understand
So much we think we know
Amazing how arrogant we are
Despite her moonlit glow

LOST TO YOU

Your memory is special to me
Don't ever doubt that you were special
Thank you for holding me
Our times together flash through my mind
And make me sad…

Your words knew me well
I didn't realize how well you knew me
I remember you telling me
that the closer you got to me
the more beautiful I became
I'm sorry I brought you so much pain.

DREAMS

Oh dreams of mine
Where have you gone?
You left me stranded,
Only half way home.
Have you no maps,
Or even an atlas,
To guide me to my destination?
The weather has been temperamental
Blizzards and rain mixed with
Sun showers
Where is my *Farmer's Almanac*
So I know how to pack for travel
You're so distant and aloof
Yet so attainable.
You're elusive and coy,
Yet so engaging
Don't toy too long
or think you will forever taunt me
I will reach you
Despite your detours.

"GOODBYE... GOODBYE"

Goodbye...goodbye;
Those words I will never forget,
For God knew, and I knew, and he knew,
That would be our last goodbye.

They ring in my ears,
They toss in my head,
They rip at my heart,
They steal my happiness away.

I said words to fill the void,
The many miles creating more helplessness,
To not be able to reach out and touch,
To end only with goodbye.

I sat alone that night,
Its memory will never fade,
It will never leave me,
For that was our goodbye.

The disease was taking him,
The foreboding in his voice told me so,
His pain that went beyond the body,
It was so clear in his goodbye.

Too few days passed before he left,
We stand around to console others,
While we writhe in our grief,
But he didn't leave without saying goodbye...goodbye.

To My Daughter

May you always know how much you are loved;
The protective arms of family forever surround you;
The love of God is always watching over you;
Keep your faith in both always close to your heart.

You have blossomed into a beautiful young woman,
Inside and out.
Your spirit of goodness which you share so generously
Holds you dearly in the hearts of others

Stay true to yourself and your faith.
Love, don't judge.
Be kind because you can't rewind.
Respect those you love and treat all gently.

You are destined for greatness.
Never underestimate yourself and what you are capable of;
Stay confident but laugh often,
Within your smile is joy and the ability
to brighten the lives of others.

I love you honey to the moon and back!
Be all you can be and keep your faith always…
Love and Hugs, Mom

CROWDED LONELINESS

Alone in my world,
Thoughts and feelings so isolating
Do not know how to feel.
In a room full of friends
Can feel so comfortable
Yet so withdrawn.

So strong, so fragile.
Life's path so unforeseen.
Battles ending in a draw
And victories fought
But never won,
And defeats that end in no resolution.

The journey is arduous,
Storms are tumultuous and rough,
The unexpected surprisingly becomes reality,
Somehow on distant, rocky shore
Is where my heart becomes home.

21

How did 21 happen so fast?
Yesterday I put you on the bus for kindergarten,
That cute little face smooshed against the window,
Saying goodbye bravely as I stood there and cried,
Letting you go to be the little man that now I realize would
grow up so quickly.
You have navigated through life with dignity and strength.
Risen to the challenges,
Undaunted, you have pursued your dreams and
let nothing stand in your way.
Your will, dedication and big heart
Have sculpted you into an admirable young man
that you have become.
May you always realize your potential within
And the blessings in store for you
For you are the artist in the masterpiece of your life.
We love you, we cherish you and feel so
blessed to have you for a son.

To My Children

As you venture off
into your future quest,
may you always know
how much you are loved, and how much you will be missed
by those who love you.

Of you we are so proud,
as should you be of yourself
Your perseverance and commitment
to your dreams and aspirations
From which you have never strayed
Will forever carry you far in life.

As you navigate your future,
May you always remember
the truth in your own heart and soul.
God is with you always.
Trust in your own judgment and instincts,
for they have always guided you well.

Be strong in character and commitment.
Endure bravely through the challenges to come.
You are stronger than you know.
Believe in yourself as we believe in you.
May your path be golden,
And your faith be strong.

Who Knew

Who knew the future to come;
the doors to open;
The windows to close,
And the promises to open wide.

Who knew the rainbow
Would be so evanescent,
But the brilliance would remain,
long after the rain dissipated.

Who knew that life and its challenges,
Could be so abrasive yet softening.
Edges that were crude and unapproachable,
Could become so refined and understanding.

Who knew
What we are capable of;
Will we ever know;
Unless we try to be there for one another.

LETTING GO OF YESTERDAY

Letting go of yesterday;
A mirage
An old reflection in the mirror;
A person who used to be;
not who stands before thee now.

Like a sandstorm
Erasing one's arduous journey in the desert;
The ocean furiously stealing away
One's travels along the beachfront.
Footprints vanishing
With every wave
Washing upon the shore.

Yesterday does not exist
in today.
Let it go
For it is gone.
Only one's memory holds it true;
In visual permanence
And emotional perspective.

Let it go if need be;
Like an annual flower
that relinquishes
to winter's harshness.

Or, an oak tree;
That continues to draw from the earth,
And grows continuously;
Like a heart that never forgets...

Let those memories
That make you soar, live on.

To My Child

Come back to the fold
Of my protective wings;
Let not your spirit be restless,
For you are here with me.
I will always be
Your one on which to lean,
Your rock, your number one fan.
Fear not child
To speak your mind;
Undo the wrongs of the day,
And together we'll make them right.
Speak of heartaches,
So that they may be subdued;
Share your joys,
So that they may be my joys too.
Always know that I am with you,
For you are my precious gift
From God.
I will always love you,
And keep you safe from life's hardships.
I will cushion your bumps,
And tend to your scrapes;
I will guide you tenderly;
Your brilliant eyes
Will always be my sun.
Share with me your heart,
And I with you.
I love you.
Mom

Too Soon Angel Wings

Presents wrapped with so much love;
Ribbons bowed with so much anticipation;
bundles of affection waiting under a tree,
Adorned with mementos of years, youth, and precious love…

Wo knew life would abandon you so young.
Your vibrancy and energy stolen away too soon;
Your brightness not to shine among us any longer,
But your memory to always live within us all.

You were so young when you earned angel wings;
Leaving us lost without you.
Emptiness filling the void that was once the vibrant you.
But from up in heaven, we know you are enjoying the view…

We miss you.
But it was your time to leave…
We love you always.
We remember you forever.

Speak Your Mind

Speak your mind
Speak your peace fully
For no one knows
What is in your heart
Unless you share it with them.

Do not assume
That they can read your thoughts
Nor know your dreams and aspirations
Without the insight of your words
And the feelings in your soul.

Life is not a passive sport
To realize one's dreams
They must be expressed
So that they may come to fruition
And not stifled by a careless onlooker.

Be strong in your beliefs
And what you can and will achieve
Let no one stand in your way
Only you define your future
With your resilience and perseverance.

LOOKING OUT UPON THE
MASSIVE BARE TREE

Its limbs reaching to the sky in all directions
Reflective of my thoughts scattered in all realms
Doubtful of myself
Have I failed or am I strong and resilient.
Have my branches splintered
Or have they remained strong to receive
my budding leaves come spring?
Have I been a sturdy enough trunk
To support and guide the extension of my offspring
I have loved so gently hard
And prayed so often.
May their branches be profuse with vibrant leaves
That reach for the sun and smile for the gentle
breeze but remain strong in storms
Reaching in all directions this powerful oak so
reminds me of life and its twists and turns
A paradigm of existence.
God? Mother Mary? Do you ever get tired of hearing from me?
I reach for you always, for guidance, for
solace, sanity, and for gratitude.
I pray thee keep me strong
So that I may keep my branches strong
And my leaves joyful.
And may the warm embrace of sunrise always remind us
That a new day dawns with a multitude of blessings,
possibilities, and dreams eager to come to fruition.

FULL CIRCLE HEALED HEART

After thirty years
I am at peace with my decision.
I saw you yesterday
And how wonderful you are
Grown into a beautiful woman
Full of life and accomplishments.
So proud of you
And all you have become.
Your life is full
Of all the love and joy
I had hoped for you
I loved spending time with you
And discovering who you are
And may there be many more occasions
Now that we have rekindled
A relationship with one another.
God bless you always
And now I think you know
How much you are loved
And how hard it was for me to let you go.
My heart is finally healed
My guilt is at rest
And for that I am so very grateful.
Shine on my beautiful daughter.
Love and hugs to you always
From my heart to yours.

About the Author

Hugs and love to all and God bless…

Liz currently resides in New Jersey with her husband of twenty-six years. She went on to have two wonderful children and experience the profound joy of being a mom. But in her heart there will always be three and August 25th of every year is a day she holds sacred when her baby girl was born.